THE ROAD BACK TO YOU

STUDY GUIDE

Five Sessions for Individuals or Groups

IAN MORGAN CRON

and

SUZANNE STABILE

IVP Books

An imprint of InterVarsity Press
Downers Grove, Illinois

InterVarsity Press
P.O. Box 1400, Downers Grove, IL 60515-1426
ivpress.com
email@ivpress.com

*InterVarsity Press® is the book-publishing division of InterVarsity Christian Fellowship/USA®, a
movement of students and faculty active on campus at hundreds of universities, colleges, and
schools of nursing in the United States of America, and a member movement of the International
Fellowship of Evangelical Students. For information about local and regional activities, visit
intervarsity.org.*

*All Scripture quotations, unless otherwise indicated, are taken from THE HOLY BIBLE, NEW
INTERNATIONAL VERSION®, NIV® Copyright © 1973, 1978, 1984, 2011 by Biblica, Inc.™ Used by
permission. All rights reserved worldwide.*

*While any stories in this book are true, some names and identifying information may have been
changed or combined to protect the privacy of individuals.*

Cover design: Cindy Kiple
Interior design: Jeanna Wiggins

ISBN 978-0-8308-4620-7 (print)
ISBN 978-0-8308-9328-7 (digital)

Printed in the United States of America ♾

Library of Congress Cataloging-in-Publication Data
A catalog record for this book is available from the Library of Congress.

P   27   26   25   24   23   22

Y   33   32   31   30   29   28   27   26   25   24   23   22   21   20

CONTENTS

INTRODUCTION

To know oneself is, above all,
to know what one lacks.

FLANNERY O'CONNOR

Welcome! Suzanne and I are so excited for you to begin this journey toward self-knowledge. In our experience there is nothing quite like the Enneagram. It describes, often with spooky accuracy, how you see and inhabit the world. It will teach you things about other people that will astound you as you learn to recognize the differences between you. It will show you the worst of you and the best of you, and help you celebrate the gifts you have. The wisdom of the Enneagram helps those who know it to understand differences, practice compassion, improve their relationships and find ways of being in the world that add meaning to their lives.

Over the next five sessions you'll learn how to determine your type and understand it in relation to other numbers. You'll also learn more about your "triad," which refers to the way that each Enneagram type is located in one

> There's great wisdom in the Enneagram for people who want to get out of their own way and move closer toward becoming the person they were created to be.

of three centers grouped around a particular way of experiencing the world: through the gut (instinct), the heart (feelings) or the head (intellect). The more you know about your own type and the types of the people you love, the more you can cultivate greater empathy and a healthier balance of all three centers.

GUIDELINES FOR THE JOURNEY

Here are a few suggestions to help you get the most from this guide over the next five weeks (or however long this takes you—feel free to take more time). First, this study guide is written so that you can go through it with a group or individually; you can either ask the questions to folks in your group or ask them to yourself privately. If you're doing the sessions alone, make sure that you are courageously and rigorously honest with yourself, since you won't have the benefit of other people to gently challenge your assumptions or self-understanding. Also, be sure not to rush. Try to devote the same amount of time each week that you would if you were part of a group and were expected to stay to the end. That's especially true for the weeks that focus on numbers besides your own. Most importantly, throughout this journey continually offer yourself the gift of self-friendship. This work and life are too hard without it.

If you are learning this material with a group, do your best to be 100 percent present. If all goes well, people in your group will open their hearts and share deeply from their lives, so give them your attention. Get to every meeting, arrive on time, stay to the end, and turn off your phone *and put it out of sight*. Be curious and open-minded about different points of view—the advantage of learning the Enneagram in a group is that you'll get to hear firsthand what it's like to see the world through the eyes of the

> Io the degree we remain ignorant of our worldview, of the messages and beliefs that for better or for worse have shaped who we are, we are prisoners of our history.

other eight numbers. Do I need to say that you must promise to maintain strict confidentiality and create a safe climate for others to share their stories and experiences without fear of exposure or judgment? Never mind, I just did.

Whether you are doing this alone or in a group, be open to changing your mind and maybe even the way you relate to the world. A pox on anyone who says, "People will have to get used to me being argumentative, I'm an Eight" or "I'll always be overly dramatic, I'm a Four." The point of learning your type is so you can relax your grip on those parts of your personality that are holding you back from living a fuller life, not so you can resign yourself to them. My spiritual director once said to me, "Insight is cheap." What he meant was information is not transformation. Knowing your number casts a light on what should stay and what you can afford to let go in your life. Knowing it's hard work will only help you grow in kindness and solidarity with others who face a similar journey.

Do You Know Your Number?

GOALS FOR THIS SESSION

- Narrow down your type, if possible
- Know the three triads
- Become familiar with SNAP (Stop, Notice, Ask, Pivot)

To read from *The Road Back to You*: chapters 1 and 2.

NARROW DOWN YOUR TYPE

Maybe you were one of those people who, when you read the chapter about Twos in *The Road Back to You*, groaned because you just *knew* you were a Two. Or maybe you were someone who said, "Some things about the Three sound familiar—I definitely focus too much on work and impressing people—but some of the aspects of the One sound like me too." Or maybe you don't have a clue yet.

Take heart: a year went by before I knew for sure that I was a Four. Regardless of whether you know your number or not, there's always more to learn about yourself, so get comfortable. Self-knowledge is a lifelong process.

In this first session, we're going to try to narrow down or confirm your type. To get started, you can look at the first three questions at the end of this session. (Each week's questions are gathered at the end of each session to facilitate your thinking and conversation.) If you need help understanding the various numbers, you may want to refer to the quick explanations of each type on pages 25 and 26 in chapter two of the book. This study guide also contains a brief overview of each number.

It can be hard to talk openly about what makes you feel uncomfortable about yourself or to come right out and say what it is you enjoy about yourself. Remember, you're in a safe place, and be sure to reinforce that feeling for others by not judging them or trying to "fix" them. And please, don't take it upon yourself to tell people what you think their number is if they aren't sure yet. You'll probably mistype and confuse them—or, worse yet, you'll guess correctly and rob them of the joy of discovering it for themselves.

> We don't know ourselves by what we get right; we know ourselves by what we get wrong. Try not to get all pouty.

No one likes a "number thumper." You've been warned.

KNOW THE THREE TRIADS

One of the ways you can help narrow down your number is to understand the three triads, or centers, that make up the Enneagram. Let's say you are in that example above, wondering whether you are a Three or a One. Your *behavior* at times could be typical of either of those numbers, which is why you need to look to your *motivations* to accurately determine your number.

Triads are helpful in getting us to understand more about why we do the things we do. In general, do you experience and process life more at the level of your gut, your heart or your head? Your Triad indicates which of the three centers (feeling, thinking, doing) you turn to first when you encounter new information or situations. The fact that you favor one of the three doesn't mean you never use the other two. Just because you're in the heart or feeling triad doesn't mean you never think or act. It's just that each of us habitually prefers one of the three centers (feeling, thinking or doing) for taking in information.

In the table below you can see at a glance which types align with which triads. As you explore this, reflect on or discuss the following questions:

1. When I encounter a new situation or problem, am I likely to want *to do* something, anything, even before I possess all of the relevant facts? (gut)

2. When I'm anxious or stressed, are people likely to tell me I'm overreacting emotionally? (heart)

3. When I'm anxious or stressed, are people likely to tell me I'm shutting down or underreacting emotionally? (head)

Thinking carefully about your dominant, default manner of reacting to situations can help you identify your triad, which can then help you narrow down your type. As you go through the sessions that follow, pay close attention to each triad's characteristics and the descriptions of each number. Don't be afraid to ask the people who know you best how they would describe your personality.

GUT TRIAD	HEART TRIAD	HEAD TRIAD
When you encounter life, your first reaction is *to do something*. • Tends to act before thinking • Anger is always waiting beneath the surface	When you encounter life, your first reaction is *to feel something*. • Tends to be overly emotional • Shame is always waiting beneath the surface	When you encounter life, your first reaction is *to think and plan*. • Tends to overthink things • Fear is always waiting beneath the surface
8: The Challenger	2: The Helper	5: The Investigator
9: The Peacemaker	3: The Performer	6: The Loyalist
1: The Perfectionist	4: The Romantic	7: The Enthusiast

INTRODUCING SNAP

The goal of understanding our number is to develop self-knowledge and learn how to recognize and relax our grip on the reflexive, self-defeating behaviors of our personalities. As we do, we can live more authentically and relate to others in wiser, more loving ways.

So how do we put to use what we've learned from the Enneagram? In the next few sessions, you'll be learning a four-movement contemplative prayer practice I first came up with to help me work with my own type. Based on the acronym SNAP (as a rule I hate acronyms too, but hang in here with me), this practice has helped me wake up to know when I've fallen back into the unhelpful patterns of thinking, feeing and acting associated with my number. It enables me to become more consciously aware of God's presence in my life here and now.

Here's how SNAP works.

Stop. Every four hours a notification comes up on my iPhone reminding me that it's time to stop for two or three minutes to give my full attention to God and to what's happening in my life at that precise moment. Sounds easy, right? Forget it. Everything in our frenzied, goal-oriented world militates against pausing even for a few minutes to switch off autopilot, and consciously come home to ourselves and to God.

But we can.

To stop, take four or five deep, prayerful breaths to ground yourself in your body and return to the present moment. If time and circumstances allow, close your eyes and scan your body from the crown of your head down to the tip of your toes. Soften any tension you encounter along the way by breathing into it. The purpose of this step is simply to wake up and bring your awareness back to your immediate experience.

Each step in the SNAP process is going to be harder for some types than others. In fact, even the act of figuring out what is challenging for you can help you zero in on your number. For example, Eights are full-speed-ahead, take-charge people. They don't like stopping or reflecting. A Nine, on the other hand, might find stopping all too easy, falling prey to distractions or even falling asleep to avoid dealing with reality. But since this is just another form of autopilot and avoidance for Nines, this is the kind of "stopping" they can learn to do without. We want the kind of stopping that can lead to greater attention to what is really going on in this moment. If we practice regularly, we'll learn to tell the difference.

Notice. Often we get swept up in the rushing river of our daily activities and habitual reactive behaviors, but rarely do we step back to observe and learn from them. Once we've come to a full stop, let's look around to see what we've been missing while we were lost in our looping thoughts or absorbed in our work. So, what's going on? Is the environment around us calm or chaotic? How are we related to what's going on? How are other people responding to us? Are we personally in a good space, or are we caught up in the default, reactive behaviors of our number?

> Not facing the reality of our darkness and its sources is a really, really bad idea.

For example, Eights practicing SNAP might realize they're feeling frustrated inside and getting ready to rip the reins of leadership out of the hands of a coworker who they think is screwing up an important project. A little awareness around that might be helpful before you act too hastily, right? Or Sixes might notice they've wasted the last two hours rehearsing in their minds what they'll say to a boss in the very unlikely event that she fires them during an upcoming annual review. Worrying that they're going to be replaced by a robot probably isn't the best use of their time.

Whatever you discover, make sure as you notice or observe what you're feeling, thinking and doing in the moment that you do so *with kindness*! No labeling, analyzing, criticizing or trying to fix anything. Simply *notice*, nothing else.

Ask. Now that you're spiritually awake and present to what's happening in the moment, you can ask yourself a few questions that will help get you back on track if you need it. In later chapters I'll suggest number-specific questions, but I found several great ones in the work of Byron Katie that I have adapted and expanded for the practice of SNAP.

1. What am I believing right now?
2. How does it make me feel?
3. Is it true?
4. Who would I be if I let go of that belief?

Imagine you're a self-aware One (the Perfectionist) and you're late for after-school pick up. Because you can tell you're a mess inside, you decide that while driving you're going to do some SNAP work (minus the "close the eyes" part). When you get to the Ask step and pose the question "What am I believing right now?" you might reflect and answer, "Right now I believe I'm the worst, most irresponsible mother in the world."

Okay, that's intense.

Now ask, "How does that feel?"

If you're a growing One, I imagine you'd saying something like, "It brings up all the old feelings of self-loathing and shame I feel every time I make mistakes." Egads, this must stop!

All right, now ask, "Is it true? Am I the worst, most irresponsible mother on the planet?" Before you scream, "Yes, I absolutely suck!" pause and think about it. *Is it really true?* You might *feel* like it is, but that doesn't make it true. Anyway, don't flatter yourself. There are plenty worse than you out there.

Now it's time to ask, "How would my life change if I let go of this belief?"

My hope is you'll say, "I'd be a happier, more relaxed and easy-going person. I might even love myself almost as much as I love the kid I'm running late to pick up right now."

Now that's better.

Pivot. In process of moving through Stop, Notice and Ask, you've exercised self-observation and deepened your self-knowledge. Armed with that, you're freed up to make different, healthier, more spiritually helpful choices in line with your true self rather than automatically defaulting to the reflexive choices you made in the past when you were half asleep on cruise control.

In the Pivot stage, we can consciously choose to throw aside the usual scripts we follow. In the example above, our One might gently inform her inner critic that rather than be all screw-faced and testy when her kid gets in the car, she's choosing to forgive herself for running behind schedule and treat them both to ice cream on the way home. She might even invite her inner critic to join them if it promises to behave.

What SNAP does is help wake us up. It interrupts the circuit on the hurtful, self-limiting thoughts, feelings and actions associated with our number and allows us to make different choices. Is it going to change your life overnight? No. But over time, it will move the needle in your self-awareness.

A FEW TIPS FOR PRACTICING SNAP

- In the beginning you might actually set a reminder on your phone or computer to remind you to practice SNAP four to five times a day until it becomes a regular discipline.

- SNAP can be done anywhere and anytime. You can devote one minute to it or a month-long retreat—either way it will benefit you.

- It's best to practice SNAP while not doing anything else, but I've done it while washing dishes, driving, raking leaves and so on.

- As you develop your attention muscles, look for spiritual practices that can help you be more aware and able at any given
  moment to see what's going on and make healthier choices.
  Centering prayer is a perfect spiritual discipline that can teach
  you to observe yourself without judgment.

- Practicing SNAP in a moment of conflict or crisis can radically
  change the course of what happens. I've practiced it at more than
  one holiday dinner when the wheels were coming off, and it's
  made all the difference.

QUESTIONS FOR REFLECTION OR DISCUSSION

1. Which of the nine types sounded *most* like you, and why?

2. Is there something about that type that makes you feel especially uncomfortable or embarrassed?

3. Is there something about that type that delights you?

4. Every triad struggles with a particular difficult emotion: the Gut
   Triad with anger, the Heart Triad with shame, and the Head
   Triad with fear. Can you think of a time in your life when you
   were dealing with the emotion that is associated with your triad?
   How did that play out?

5. Which of the four stages of SNAP do you think will be most challenging for you? Is it more difficult for you to *stop* what you're doing, *notice* your patterns of behavior, *ask* questions of yourself or *pivot* to change your conduct?

6. What is a default behavior that you employ when you are feeling anxious or stressed? In what ways is this behavior healthy or unhealthy?

7. Think about this quote from the book: "We don't know ourselves by what we get right; we know ourselves by what we get wrong." Can you remember a time when your darker side taught you something important about yourself?

8. Have you ever tried centering prayer or another form of meditation? If so, how did it feel? (If you are interested in centering prayer and would like to know more, I suggest reading *Open Mind, Open Heart* by Fr. Thomas Keating or *Into the Silent Land* by Martin Laird.)

Reading for next week: chapters 3, 4 and 5 of *The Road Back to You.*

The Gut Triad (8, 9 and 1)

GOALS FOR THIS SESSION

- Understand Type 8 (The Challenger)
- Understand Type 9 (The Peacemaker)
- Understand Type 1 (The Perfectionist)

To read from *The Road Back to You*: chapters 3, 4 and 5.

Welcome back! In this session we'll meet the numbers that make up the Gut Triad—Eights, Nines and Ones. We'll explore each number's deadly sin and introduce their "contrary virtues." As I mentioned in the introduction, the side benefit of learning each number's deadly sin is that it can help people nail down their type. Any doubt I had that I was a Four was immediately swept aside the moment I learned their deadly sin is envy.

If you already know your number and its deadly sin, then learning about its contrary virtue will provide you with insight to the work you have ahead of you.

Next, we'll dive in and look at the world through the lenses of Eights, Nines and Ones. This is a great time for those in your group who identify as one of these numbers to share how they see and experience the world.

Remember that we should only use what we know about other people's numbers to encourage and free them, never to dismiss or make fun of them. Rolling your eyes and saying things like "You're such a Six" is verboten.

THE SINS AND VIRTUES OF THE GUT TRIAD

Type	8	9	1
Deadly Sin to Avoid	*Lust.* Eights are intense, excessive people who want to be in control and project strength to mask weakness or vulnerable feelings.	*Sloth.* Nines are spiritually lazy people who merge with the priorities, values and preferences of others to avoid conflict and maintain inner peace.	*Anger.* Ones compulsively strive to perfect the world and become chronically resentful toward those who cannot live up to their standards, particularly themselves.
Countering Virtue to Cultivate	*Chastity.* Eights can moderate their intensity, excessiveness and need for control and recognize the value of vulnerability.	*Diligence.* Nines can assert themselves and self-actualize through consciously pursuing their life's agenda, even if it arouses conflict and their fear of disconnection.	*Patience.* Ones can learn to accept that there's more than one way to do things and have more patience with the world—and themselves—for being imperfect.

TYPE EIGHT

Hear What Eights Have to Say

What I like about being an Eight:

The best thing about being an Eight is the innate confidence we possess. We can make things happen and get things done. We simply *know* that we can do "it"—whether that's launching a business, running for office, leading a group toward a goal or baking a cake. We got this. —Heather H.

What I don't like about being an Eight:

Eights can be tone deaf to all the unspoken feelings, fears and biases of other people. Thus, many times I excitedly push forward with the stated goals and objectives of a group, only to realize that I am the jerk (and all alone) because I didn't hang back with the rest of the not-quite-ready-to-actually-do-anything group. Eights can be perceived as insensitive and judged as bossy or challenging. —Christine M.

What I wish people understood about being an Eight:

Don't take how I am in the world personally. My aggressive stance is not about you, and you don't need to be afraid or concerned that it is. —Jeff

QUESTIONS TO HELP YOU FIGURE OUT WHETHER YOU ARE AN EIGHT

1. Do you feel comfortable taking charge in a group?
2. Are you known for your ability and willingness to take a stand?
3. Do you get annoyed when other people are indirect or manipulative, or can't seem to state what they really mean or want?
4. Do you have a hard time letting down your guard or allowing other people to see you in a weak moment?
5. Are other people sometimes intimidated by your tendency to bring conflict out into the open and by your aggressive nature?
6. Do you tend to value being respected more than being liked?
7. Is it difficult for you to trust people?

SNAP IDEAS FOR EIGHTS

Stop. Stop. *Literally* stop. If possible, put down whatever you're doing and for the next few minutes cease all troop movements. Breathe. Find your center and ground yourself in the present. Whoa, that's hard for an Eight.

Most Eights don't welcome or enjoy times of self-reflection. Tender, softer feelings are more apt to arise when a person powers down—and moving targets are harder to hit than those that are sitting still.

Notice. Look around you. What's happening? Is your body tensed or relaxed? Are you speaking normally or loudly? Do people appear to be relaxed around you or like they're walking on eggshells?

If you're out, is your walking gait relaxed, or are you charging forward with your chest thrust out in front of you? How many demands are you placing on your body right now? Are you overworking it, tired? Are you over-indulging or being excessive in some way?

> What feels like intimidation to you feels like intimacy to an Eight.

Now observe your feelings. If you notice you're feeling angry or "overcharged," see whether you can sense softer feelings somewhere underneath it. Should tender feelings reveal themselves, be sure not to judge them as signs of weakness.

Can you notice whether you're pushing against something or someone? Who or what is it?

Ask. As you learn more about your number and the unique way you inhabit it, you'll come up with questions specifically applicable to you. These four questions are always great.

1. What am I believing right now? That the world is a heartless and unjust place and I need to be battle-ready at all times? That I need to be strong and in control or else I or someone I care about will get hurt? That opening my heart to others always leads to betrayal and emotional harm?

2. What does this belief lead me to feel? Guarded? Suspicious? Defensive? Like I have to maintain a display of strength to ward off would-be attackers?

3. Is it true? Is everyone untrustworthy and out to take advantage of the weak? Do I always need to be strong and in control? Is it even possible? Is this *really* true?

4. What would happen if I let go of that belief? Would people begin to respond to me with love and not just respect? Would I be able to relax and let go of needing to be in charge?

Pivot. For an Eight, pivoting might mean

- Thinking and feeling before you act
- Opening your heart to someone
- Allowing things to happen rather than making them happen
- Letting others lead you
- Walking more slowly and smiling more

Practice chastity, the contrary virtue to lust, by exercising moderation and channeling your energy toward positive ends.

※   ※   ※

TYPE NINE

Hear What Nines Have to Say

What I like about being a Nine:

The best thing is that I'm available to people when we're together. And—from an Eight daughter's perspective—they get to do what they want to do! —Debbie T.

What I don't like about being a Nine:

For Nines it is really hard to hear the message that we matter. Any compliment I have gotten my entire life was instantly undercut and dismissed by six different ways in which it was not true or was patronizing. In order for Nines to receive the message that they matter requires acts which cannot be denied. —Wade M.

A Nine-ish behavior:

It's hard to lean into my own confidence and power. I can attach to other people's power and be supportive, but taking the lead is hard. There's lots of anxiety and second guessing. —Charlie L.

What I wish people understood about being a Nine:

That we behave like a duck: calm on the surface but paddling like crazy underneath. —Debbie T.

QUESTIONS TO HELP YOU FIGURE OUT WHETHER YOU ARE A NINE

1. Are you usually able to see multiple points of view, making it harder to know and choose where you stand?

2. Are you easily distracted, daunted by the prospect of focusing single-mindedly on the task that is right in front of you?

3. Do you often choose the easiest way out of a problem, especially if it avoids potential conflict or an argument?

4. Do you employ passive-aggressive strategies when people are too demanding (like "forgetting" about commitments you agreed to but didn't actually want to do, or falling asleep to avoid attending to reality)?

5. Do you see other people's opinions as carrying more weight than your own?

6. Do other people see you as easygoing and free of worry, even if that's not true of how you feel inside?

7. Is it hard for you to prioritize and accomplish the things you are supposed to do in a given day?

> Nines know how to rest in God's love and share themselves more generously than the rest of us.

SNAP IDEAS FOR NINES

Stop. For Nines, stopping is a breeze. You're a body-centered person, so you know how to get grounded in your breath and come home to yourself when you're encouraged or in the habit of doing it. For Nines, it's stopping and *remaining focused and alert* in the present moment that's hard.

Notice. What's going on around you? At this moment how engaged with life are you? Are you tuned in to what's happening or tuned out? Are you present and accounted for or missing in action? Are you letting life *get to you*?

Notice whether conflict is present or threatening and how you're responding. Are you avoiding it? If so, how?

To avoid conflict, are you merging? Are you setting aside your preferences, opinions, wants, desires and agenda to avoid rocking the boat?

Are you staying on task, focusing on doing what needs to be done, or have you lost sight of the big picture and the capacity to prioritize?

Are you numbing anger or resentment through vegging out, feeding addictive behaviors, or getting lost in habits and routines that require no thought?

Notice whether you're somehow expressing anger or displeasure through stubbornness, avoidance or other passive-aggressive behaviors.

Ask.

1. What am I believing right now? That I'm unimportant? That I have to sacrifice my own desires to maintain connection to others? That I can't handle conflict? That something terrible will happen if I get in touch with my anger or express it?

2. How does that make me feel? Resentful? Frustrated? Numb? Exhausted?

3. Is what I'm believing right now true? Does my presence really not matter? Would I not survive conflict? Are my own dreams and priorities unimportant? Is this *really* true?

4. What if let go of this belief? Would I find and lay claim to my voice? Would I grow in self-respect and self-regard?

Pivot.

- Express your anger directly.
- Tell others what you want.

- Wake up and engage with whatever's next.
- Acknowledge your value and assert yourself.
- Talk and let others listen.
- Make a list and stick to it.

The contrary virtue to sloth is diligence. Determine your priorities and commit to an action plan to accomplish them.

⁄⁄⁄   ⁄⁄⁄   ⁄⁄⁄

TYPE ONE

Hear What Ones Have to Say

What I like about being a One:

I am dependable and punctual. I have strong ethics and high standards. I am very good with details. —Julianne H.

What I don't like about being a One:

That I see what is wrong or needs fixing as soon as I enter a room or situation.

Not only do I notice it, but I have this strong drive to *name* all that needs fixing first, before I allow myself to move on to what is good and blessed and beautiful. Can you imagine? Who wants to be around someone who's always quick to point out what's wrong? And because I'm a naturally optimistic, fun-loving person, I hate how I feel about *myself* when I give into this urge. —Mary L.

A One-ish behavior:

When my kids are told to pick up their rooms I go in and point out what they missed. It has been very frustrating for them. My heart isn't intending to criticize, but to teach and improve. I am always going to try to make it better. —Julianne C.

What I wish people understood about being a One:

I wish people knew that I take any criticism, even constructive criticism, as confirmation that the "Voice" is correct and I am really not good enough. I also wish they knew that my intention is not to hurt people when I suggest ways they could improve. —Julianne H.

QUESTIONS TO HELP YOU FIGURE OUT WHETHER YOU ARE A ONE

1. Does it bother you a lot when other people try to bend the rules to their own advantage, and the rules don't seem to be the same for everyone across the board?

2. Do you almost always give 100 percent to a task and expect other people to do the same? (And if they don't, are you likely to come along after they've finished and do their work all over again just to get it right?)

3. Are you concerned about fixing what's not working in the world, and do you feel a personal responsibility to change things?

4. Are you a judgmental person? And does your inner critic attack your own efforts most of all?

5. Are you more likely than other people to notice mistakes or things being out of place?

6. Are you a self-disciplined, detail-oriented person?

7. Is it hard for you to forgive others and let go of past wrongs?

SNAP IDEAS FOR ONES

Stop. As someone who is a "doer," stopping even for a few minutes will be difficult for you. You might resent the interruption when the reminder to practice SNAP pops up, but take a breath and do it.

As you work through each step in SNAP be sure to practice compassion toward yourself.

Resist the temptation to procrastinate beginning this practice because you're afraid of making mistakes. A rule in contemplative prayer is that everyone who shows up gets an A+. Don't harshly judge yourself, worry about whether you're doing it right or fret over whether you're properly following the directions.

> If you want someone who is efficient, ethical, meticulous, reliable and does the work of two people, then hire a One!

Notice. When noticing what's going on externally and internally, your attention will naturally be drawn to what's not right or appropriate. If this happens, simply observe without judgment that this too is part of your experience. As a One, make sure as you notice not only the things that are wrong but also two or three things that are right.

Ask. As you learn more and more about your personality and the unique way you inhabit it, I encourage you to come up with your own questions more suited to your particular needs. Here are a few sample answers to the four questions I proposed you could use anytime.

1. What are you believing right now? That you are obligated to correct error in others and in the environment? That it's unacceptable for you to make mistakes? That your inner critic speaks with the authority of God?

2. How does this belief make you feel? (Resist the temptation to reject owning feelings you consider "inappropriate.") Are you feeling angry or resentful right now? Worried you'll be blamed or criticized for making a mistake? Like you're fighting a losing battle against reality?

3. Is it true? Are you actually responsible for perfecting the world? Are things always right or wrong, good or bad, black or white? Is your way the only right way of doing things? Is this *really* true?

4. How would your life be different if you let go of this belief? How would it feel to be able to hold the space not only of either-or but both/and as well? Would your inner critic speak less harshly and loudly? Would you kick off your shoes and let yourself have more fun?

   Pivot.

- Memorize the opening lines of the Serenity Prayer and recite it aloud. Couldn't be more right for you. "God, grant me the serenity to accept the things I cannot change, the courage to change the things I can, and the wisdom to know the difference."

- Accept mistakes as a natural occurrence in everyone's life.

- Remind yourself that every person is inherently worthy.

- Do something fun. If your inner critic says frivolity is out of the question because there's too much to do, tell it that it can come with you or stay home, but either way you're doing this.

- Remind your inner critic how much you appreciate its role in helping you as a kid but now invite it to shift from the role of taskmaster to encouraging guide.

- Intentionally make a mistake or do something imperfectly or incompletely. Go to bed without doing the dishes. Run 2.8 miles rather than 3 on the nose. Yes, that's what I said.

Find ways to practice the virtue of patience, which is the contrary virtue to your deadly sin of anger.

⁂ ⁂ ⁂

QUESTIONS FOR REFLECTION AND DISCUSSION

If you are participating in a group that is discussing the Enneagram, it's important that you take the time to truly listen to

what participants of other numbers have to say about themselves.
Try to see the world through their eyes if possible. Allow them to
speak without interruption. If you are going through this guide on
your own, take time to reflect and journal through each question.
Reflect on what it's like to be each number. The Enneagram is a
great tool for developing empathy and compassion.

1. In this session we have been looking at the Gut Triad: the Challenger, the Peacemaker and the Perfectionist. If you are one of
   these three types, does the idea of reacting to life "from the gut"
   resonate with you? Why or why not?

2. Do the deadly sins associated with these numbers (lust for
   Eights, sloth for Nines and anger for Ones) ring true to you? If
   yes, how? If not, why? What are spiritual practices that can cultivate the counterbalancing virtue for each deadly sin?

3. For Eights, Nines and Ones: What do you like most about
   your number?

4. For Eights, Nines and Ones: What do you like least about your number?

5. For Eights, Nines and Ones: What do you wish people understood about your number?

6. For people of the other six numbers: What do you most appreciate or envy about Eights, Nines and Ones?

7. For people of the other six numbers: What drives you crazy about Eights, Nines and Ones?

Reading for next week: chapters 6, 7 and 8 of *The Road Back to You.*

THE HEART TRIAD (2, 3 AND 4)

GOALS FOR THIS SESSION

- Understand Type 2 (The Helper)
- Understand Type 3 (The Performer)
- Understand Type 4 (The Romantic)

To read from *The Road Back to You*: chapters 6, 7 and 8.

THE SINS AND VIRTUES OF THE HEART TRIAD

Type	2	3	4
Deadly Sin to Avoid	*Pride.* Twos secretly believe other people have more needs than they do and would be lost without their help.	*Deceit.* To satisfy their craving for admiration, Threes project crowd-pleasing images that deceive even themselves.	*Envy.* Fours believe they lack an essential element and will never have the wholeness others enjoy. They envy the normalcy and happiness of others.
Countering Virtue to Cultivate	*Humility.* Twos can develop humility when they acknowledge their own needs and ask others directly for their help and support.	*Integrity.* By discovering and sharing their true selves with others, Threes learn they are loved for who they are and not for what they do.	*Gratitude.* Fours counteract envy when they dwell not on what's missing but on what's present in the way of their gifts and blessings.

TYPE TWO

Hear What Twos Have to Say

What I like about being a Two:

I nearly always know how to respond and behave in complicated social situations (e.g., being in the room as someone is being told a devastating medical diagnosis). —Hunter M.

What I don't like about being a Two:

I desperately want people to give me positive feedback and compliments, but once they do, I can't enjoy them, because it feels too exposing to have the attention focused on my needs and behaviors. —Hunter M.

What I wish other people understood about being a Two:

Being a Two as a wife and mother can be a double bind. Society rewards us for caring for others and putting our loved ones before ourselves. As caretakers it is expected, and something most women do naturally. I find the line between what is expected of me and who I am as a Two to be blurred. —Lisa H.

QUESTIONS TO HELP YOU FIGURE OUT WHETHER YOU ARE A TWO

1. Are you a people-pleaser, ready to drop your own concerns in order to help others?

2. Is it painful or embarrassing for you to ask other people for help?

3. Are you especially attuned to the feelings of others?

4. Are you known as an excellent listener, the first person your friends go to when they need a shoulder to cry on?

5. Do you place a value on making your home a comfortable place for people to find refuge?

6. Is it frustrating for you when the people you love need to be told what you need, instead of just intuiting it?

7. Are you typically the first to apologize and to forgive?

SNAP IDEAS FOR TWOS

Stop. For Twos, it's hard to stop, especially if it means having to relationally disconnect to do it. It's a challenge to focus inward when your focus is always outward. It feels unnatural for you to stop to care for yourself.

Notice. As you look around, see whether you feel tempted to move toward another person near you. Ask yourself, *Am I feeling unappreciated and resentful at the moment? Am I feeling taken for granted? Am I pretending to love someone right now? Is there a place on my body where I seem to bottle up tension?*

> Twos can walk into a party and intuit which couple had a fight on the way over, who would rather be home watching baseball and which person is anxious about losing her job.

Ask. As you learn more and more about your personality and the unique way you inhabit it, I encourage you to come up with your own questions more suited to your particular needs.

1. What am I believing right now? That I have to meet the needs of others to be loved? That the needs of others are more important than my own? That I'm indispensable? That I have an endless supply of resources to address the needs of others?

2. How does holding on to this belief make me feel? Prideful? Needed? Resentful? Sad? Spent? Unable to articulate my own needs and wants? (Don't be surprised if you're uncertain about how it makes you feel. As a Two, you spend so much time focusing outwardly on the feelings of others you're only now becoming familiar with your own.)

3. Is it true that to be loved I need to meet the needs of others? Is it true that if I'm seen for who I am I'll be rejected? Is this *really* true?

4. How would my life be different if I let go of this belief? Would I be able to acknowledge and address my own needs? Would I no longer need to exhaust myself pleasing other people? Would I be able to love and take care of myself as much as I love and take care of others?

Pivot.

- Pay attention to what you need.

- Think before you do!

- Receive from others.

- When someone asks you to do something, practice saying, "Let me think about it and get back to you" or "No."

- Resist projecting the image of the cheerful, likable helper. Are you in this mode right now? If so, can you make a different choice?

- Remind yourself, "Love is an inside job."

- To get a start on cultivating humility, which is the contrary virtue to pride, acknowledge and directly express a need to someone.

※   ※   ※

TYPE THREE

Hear What Threes Have to Say

What I like about being a Three:

I love the feeling of being an energizer bunny. —Jon S.

What I don't like about being a Three:

Seeking approval. I was involved in Girl Scouting all throughout my childhood, earning all of the awards and achieving the highest ranks. I didn't really love Scouting and rarely, if ever, talked about my Scouting involvement or achievements with any of my other groups of friends. Scouting was incredibly influential in my mother's childhood and adolescence and she was always very, very glad that I had stayed involved. I've come to realize I was never particularly interested in Scouting myself, I just wanted the assurance of relationship that came from knowing I was involved in something that pleased my mother. —Laura A.

I'm not sure how to describe my relationships to feelings. When asked what I'm feeling I run out of words very quickly. —Wade

A Three-ish behavior:

Soon after I began working professionally, I sat in a bullpen arrangement of desks without dividing walls so everyone could hear each other. After hanging up the phone one day, a coworker said, "Do you know you sound like a completely different person with every person you talk to?" I was taken aback. That seemed disingenuous of me. She had to be wrong. That sensation lasted all of about twelve seconds because quickly another person in the room chimed in, "Yeah, you do that, Brian." I learned some years later that this skill of being who you need to be in order to communicate is called "matching." Basically you automatically become whoever you need to be based on the client. I've never had a job where this ability wasn't highly sought and highly praised. It sounds good, but I have to keep up with who I am with any number of persons, and that's hard to do. Am I the affable guy from the river valley when I talk to Mike, or am I the stuck-up blueblood with him? Who can keep up? —Brian I.

What I wish other people understood about being a Three:

One thing people don't understand about Threes is that we don't just want to be the best, but we want it to look easy. —Josh

QUESTIONS TO HELP YOU FIGURE OUT WHETHER YOU ARE A THREE

1. Are you restless and bored unless you have a clear goal to achieve?
2. Is it important to you to be perceived by friends and colleagues as successful?
3. Do you have a chameleon-like ability to adapt your personality to the situation you're in and the expectations of the people around you?
4. Are you more afraid of failure than you let on?
5. Can you turn your emotions off like a spigot in order to attend to your work?
6. Do you crave the spotlight and the approval of others?
7. Are you skilled at promoting yourself and making a great first impression?

> Threes have a supernatural talent for multitasking. They can simultaneously juggle driving, closing a multimillion-dollar deal on their cell phone, eating a sandwich, listening to an audiobook, and conversing with their spouse about a problem one of the kids is having at school.

SNAP IDEAS FOR THREES

Stop. As a Three, having to stop to do anything that deflects your attention away from work or any other goal-directed activity will feel like an unwanted interruption. Resist the temptation to believe there's less payoff for working on your interior world than on your exterior one. If necessary, *set a goal* of faithfully practicing SNAP for thirty days and see how it goes from there.

Notice. Look around you. Are you currently running over people to reach a goal? For the sake of efficiency are you cutting corners? At this moment are you comparing yourself to others?

Turning your attention internally, are you currently feeling pressure to re-invent yourself to win recognition and applause?

Are you setting feelings aside to avoid slowing down work?

Even if you're unsure of the answer, it's great practice for Threes to simply ask the question, "What am I feeling right now?"

Ask. As you learn more and more about your personality and the unique way you inhabit it, I encourage you to come up with your own questions more suited to your particular needs.

1. What am I believing right now? That my value is proportional to my accomplishments and success? That I have to be the best at everything? That I have to project an image to match the values and preferences of my audience?

2. How does this belief make me feel? Lonely? Excited? Like a fraud? Like a rock star?

3. Is it true that before I can be loved I need to be a star? Is status really everything? Is it reasonable for me to believe there's no one behind my mask? Is it *really* true?

4. How would my life be different if I believed I could be loved apart from anything I do? That it's okay to have my own feelings and identity apart from what I think others expect of me?

Pivot.

• If you're projecting one of your successful images at this moment to win recognition, relax it.

• If you're currently spinning a negative situation into a positive so you can avoid the appearance of failure, stop and tell the truth.

• Have that heart-to-heart conversation you know you need to have with someone important in your life even though it will involve messy feelings.

• Try to discipline yourself not to work after 6 p.m.

• Avoid reducing life to tasks.

• Allow your feelings to arise and affect you.

- Value relationships over goals.
- Slow down.

  Cultivate integrity, the contrary virtue to your deadly sin of deceit.

※   ※   ※

TYPE FOUR

Hear What Fours Have to Say

What I like about being a Four:

Being a safe place for people to share themselves. —Judy B.

I am able to use my emotional sensitivity and observation skills to connect in very meaningful ways with my loved ones, friends, colleagues and young students. For me there is nothing as beautiful as the landscape of intimacy, growth and development! —Michelle J.

What I don't like about being a Four:

I used to wonder why I was drawn to fundamentalism as a kid if I'm a Four. It explained what was missing, what was broken, why others and the world are broken. But the answer doesn't satisfy forever. —Don C.

Fours need to work on envy—anyone can tell me anything and I'd think if I had that, did that or had the talent to do it I wouldn't have this missing piece. If you told me you just went to Slovenia I would think a trip to Slovenia would be just what I needed to self-actualize. —Lennijo

A Four-ish behavior:

When I was growing up, my mom hated shopping with me. When we would go back-to-school shopping in August, for example, she thought it should be a simple trip where we just needed to find a few shirts, a couple pairs of pants and a new pair of shoes that would fit me and fit the dress code. This very utilitarian, practical view did not jive with my aesthetic sensibilities because I already knew *exactly* what I wanted. I had already pictured in my mind's eye exactly what those shirts, pants, shoes and a few accessories should look like, and I wouldn't settle for anything less than what I had imagined. I was otherwise a very sweet, accommodating child and later teenager, but on this I was unyielding. By the end of the shopping trip, my mom would be begging me to buy something, *anything*, so we could be done, and I rarely relented. It seemed very important to me to express myself through my clothing, and I would never wear something generic. —Lucy S.

What I wish other people understood about being a Four:

I feel things really deeply, so people see someone who is emotional and sometimes sensitive and think I must be timid and delicate. But I think the depth of my emotions makes me really strong and resilient, even if the kind of resiliency I have is different than that of an Eight or another number. It ain't easy going through life feeling all of the feelings, and it has forced me to learn how to take care of myself and build up fortitude. I would love for people to know that being sensitive and tender does not preclude being strong, competent and capable. —Lucy S.

QUESTIONS TO HELP YOU FIGURE OUT WHETHER YOU ARE A FOUR

1. Are you driven to be special and unique, noticeably different from other people?
2. Do your emotions sometimes engulf you? Are your moods characterized by the highest highs and the lowest lows?

3. Do you spend a good deal of time dwelling on the past?

4. Do you appreciate sad movies, books or songs? Do tragic stories strike a deep chord within you?

5. Do you feel like all your life you've been searching for a "missing piece" that would complete you?

6. Do you have an intense push-pull dynamic in your relationships, where you alternate between being passionate and being withdrawn?

7. Are you envious of other people's success, relationships or happiness?

> Fours are the most complex of all the types on the Enneagram; what you see is never what you get.

SNAP IDEAS FOR FOURS

Stop. As a naturally introspective type who easily connects with your feelings, you won't have trouble stopping to self-reflect. If anything, you might get sucked into your emotions and have trouble moving forward to the next steps. Don't think I don't know. I'm a Four.

Notice. Step out of and observe your feelings. What are they? Are you having them or are they having you?

As you look around, can you detect whether there's a drama underway? As you observe it, ask yourself whether you're contributing to it. Are you using your rich imagination to embellish or intensify your feelings?

Are you lost in dreams about an ideal future or ruminating over a tragic past right now? Are you longing for the unavailable? Are you in the grip of melancholy?

Ask.

1. What am I believing right now? Do I believe I'm missing something everyone else has that makes me an outsider? Do I feel I need to be special to compensate or cover up my inner lack?

2. How does this belief make me feel? (As someone who over-
identifies with your feelings, be careful not to spend too much
time on this step or you'll never move off it to the next one.)

3. Is this belief true? Am I my feelings? Am I really missing something essential in my makeup? If so, what is it?

4. How would my life be different if I let go of this belief? Would I
be okay if the answer was that I'd become more of a regular,
ordinary person? Would I feel relieved that I didn't have to try
so hard to be unique or special all the time?

Pivot.

• If you're up to your nose in feelings, repeatedly remind yourself,
"No emotion is final."

• Being unique doesn't make you useful. Focus more on being the
latter, not the former.

• Take action. What wildly creative dream have you been fanta-
sizing about but procrastinating on that you can begin right now?

• If you're dwelling on the past and running the old "If only . . .
If only . . . If only . . ." script, break the trance by thanking God
for the here and now and the future he has for you. Then turn
your attention to doing something productive.

• Put a Post-it note somewhere you'll see it with the words,
"Nothing's missing" or "Everything I need to be content is here."
Initially you might not believe it, but over time it will break
through your resistance.

• Appreciate life as it is.

• Focus outward.

• Accept that emotional intensity is not a prerequisite for emotional fulfillment.

Cultivate the contrary virtue of gratitude to help you overcome
your deadly sin of envy.

※   ※   ※

QUESTIONS FOR REFLECTION AND DISCUSSION

If you are participating in a group that is discussing the Enneagram, it's important that you take the time to truly listen to what participants of other numbers have to say about themselves. Try to see the world through their eyes if possible. Allow them to speak without interruption. If you are going through this guide on your own, take time to reflect and journal through each question. Reflect on what it's like to be each number. The Enneagram is a great tool for developing empathy and understanding.

1. In this session we have been looking at the Heart Triad: the Helper, the Performer and the Romantic. If you are one of these three types, does the idea of leading with your heart or feelings resonate with you? Why or why not?

2. Do the deadly sins associated with these numbers (pride for Twos, deceit for Threes and envy for Fours) ring true to you? What are spiritual practices that can counterbalance these deadly sins?

3. For Twos, Threes and Fours: What do you like most about your number?

4. For Twos, Threes and Fours: What do you like least about your number?

5. For Twos, Threes and Fours: What do you wish people understood about your number?

6. For people of the other six numbers: What do you most appreciate or envy about Twos, Threes and Fours?

7. For people of the other six numbers: What drives you crazy about Twos, Threes and Fours?

Reading for next week: chapters 9, 10 and 11 of *The Road Back to You.*

THE HEAD TRIAD (5, 6 AND 7)

GOALS FOR THIS SESSION

- Understand Type 5 (The Investigator)
- Understand Type 6 (The Loyalist)
- Understand Type 7 (The Enthusiast)

To read from *The Road Back to You*: chapters 9, 10 and 11.

THE SINS AND VIRTUES OF THE HEAD TRIAD

Type	5	6	7
Deadly Sin to Avoid	*Avarice.* Afraid they lack the inner resources to meet the demands of life and to preserve independence and energy, Fives hoard knowledge, privacy, time, space and affection.	*Fear.* Needing to feel secure, Sixes rehearse worst-case scenarios and seek out and attach to strong authority figures and belief systems.	*Gluttony.* To avoid feelings of pain and chronic deprivation, Sevens compulsively plan and gluttonously devour exciting experiences, fascinating ideas and the best life has to offer.
Countering Virtue to Cultivate	*Generosity.* Fives become generous when they relax their mindset of scarcity and embrace the reality of abundance.	*Faith.* Sixes can develop faith that renders worst-case-scenario planning unnecessary and learn to trust their inner compass to guide them in making good decisions.	*Sobriety.* For Sevens sobriety means exercising self-restraint, accepting and integrating both the joys and sorrows of life, and following through on long-term commitments with projects and people.

TYPE FIVE

Hear What Fives Have to Say

What I like about being a Five:

When I walk my dog down my county road, I take in the natural beauty along my path. I pause to view in each direction multiple times. I study the images: lush grass, brilliant flowers, fresh leafy trees. Wow. This is what a Five can do so well: observe, ponder, feel without anything else. My thoughts can lead me to extreme joy. I don't need anyone else to feel that good. —B. N.

What I don't like about being a Five:

The worst thing about my number is my disruptive reaction to unpredictable events or unexpected interruptions. I often react with angry outbursts to the most innocent intrusion. When I want to do something, I can ignore my physical body and I feel like I have unlimited energy. However, if someone asks me to do something, I become a time miser, counting every second of that interruption. —Dale R.

A Five-ish behavior:

A midnight caller said, "Your father is not breathing. Please come. Paramedics are with him now." I ended the call, calmly dressed, thoughtfully selected some supplies for the long night ahead, and quietly drove to Dad's assisted-living memory care facility. A police car, not an ambulance, was parked at the entrance. All was eerily quiet. I learned my father had died and a policeman interviewed me for a while. I responded in a professional manner to each question. In my mind I thought, "Holy cow, my dad just died and I'm standing here calmly answering questions? Where are my emotions!?" —B. N.

What I wish other people understood about being a Five:

The most difficult thing about being a five is being misunderstood in relational situations because of my detached and perceived aloofness. —Ken B.

QUESTIONS TO HELP YOU FIGURE OUT WHETHER YOU ARE A FIVE

1. Do you tend to "keep yourself to yourself," sharing your deepest emotions and thoughts with only a very few people?
2. Do you tend to need time to process new experiences and emotions?
3. When you are in a group, would you rather observe than participate?
4. If given the choice of staying home to watch a movie or going to a party with people you don't yet know well, are you inclined to stay home?
5. Do you feel drained after spending too much time in the company of other people?
6. Do you prefer to make decisions with your head instead of your heart?
7. Are you wondering why in the world you agreed to come to this discussion group that is all about *feelings*? (Or are you doing this study guide at home alone because the thought of such a discussion group makes your hair hurt?)

SNAP IDEAS FOR FIVES

Stop. SNAP might be an easier practice for you than it is for any other number. You're a natural contemplative so I'm not worried about you stopping to do it.

Notice. Your superpower is observing life in a detached, nonjudgmental, analytical manner. Noticing is your strong suit. The key here will be to avoid only observing others to the exclusion of observing yourself.

Here are some things you might look for as you observe: Are you present in your body or one step removed from it right now? Do you observe yourself feeling exasperated with people because they're not staying on task or topic?

Are you acting a bit like Dr. House (a very unhealthy Five!) because you believe you're superior to others or justified in talking down to them because of the impressive amount of information you have accumulated and the depth of knowledge you possess in your area of expertise?

> How different would Fives' lives be if they embraced a mindset of abundance?

Do you observe yourself feeling incapable or incompetent or overly concerned about not having an answer to something and looking foolish?

Are you holed up collecting information to avoid having to make contact with others?

Ask. As you learn more and more about your personality and the unique way you inhabit it, I encourage you to come up with your own questions more suited to your particular needs.

1. What is it I am believing right now? That I don't have the resources to manage life like other people? I'm socially awkward? I don't have the energy for this meeting or encounter and I have to leave? That I'm inferior (or superior) because I see things so differently from others? That there's no seat at the table for me?

2. How does this belief make me feel? (As the most emotionally detached number on the Enneagram you tend to try to think your way to your feelings or postpone having them until you've had time to analyze them, which can take too much time. So answer this question with the first thing that comes up when

you ask it. Give it your best then open yourself to actually having that feeling. It will take time.)

3. Is it true that I don't have the resources to cope to meet the demands of life? Is it *really* true?

4. What would my life be like if I let go of this belief? Would I be more emotionally available to connect to the people I care about? Would I be less fearful about looking inept or foolish? Would I find myself allowing feelings to rise in the moment?

Pivot.

- If you are being unnecessarily private or stingy with love or affection, actually open up to someone who you know wants to love and support you.

- Let go of any hurt you may have over someone disagreeing with one of your ideas.

- Don't observe life; participate in it.

- Expand your feelings by connecting to them.

- Practice being present when you are with people.

- To counterbalance your deadly sin of avarice, cultivate the virtue of generosity.

※   ※   ※

TYPE SIX

Hear What Sixes Have to Say

What I like about being a Six:

If you give me a steak, I will return to you a cow. We are very loyal and giving. We appreciate and respect our friendships.
—Lynn T.

What I don't like about being a Six:

One of the worst things about my number is the tendency to feel overwhelmed and stressed and then want to shut down and not act or think productively. When something is overwhelming or stressful I want to put it off until the last possible minute. I can hem and haw and doubt my feelings and desires. One of the biggest things I have had to learn is how to face my fears and indecision and not let them paralyze me. —Joy P.

A Six-ish behavior:

I think I knew as a child that not everyone stayed awake at night thinking about the band test the next day. I was aware that my anxiety was different, and that I was more aware than other people. I sensed when people in the room were left out and needed a friend. I sensed when someone wanted my dad to stop talking to them, even when he didn't. My radar was picking up things I realized other people never noticed. Yet the anxiety was like a dark secret. I don't think anyone would have known how anxious I really was about certain things, even my own family. I kept it so hidden, and I felt so alone in the pain. —Jane

What I wish other people understood about being a Six:

When I ask you a question, I just want an honest, truthful answer to the question I asked, not to the question you wish I asked or information about something relative to what I asked. I don't want a story. I don't want to be blown off or put off. I don't want to irritate, embarrass, intimidate or threaten you. I just want a truthful, factual answer. If you can't give it or don't know it, that's OK, just say so, but don't lie or get angry or avoid me, because I will stay in pursuit until I get the answer. —Dana E.

QUESTIONS TO HELP YOU FIGURE OUT WHETHER YOU ARE A SIX

1. Once you form a bond with someone, are you likely to do whatever it takes to preserve that bond in the years to come?

2. Do you typically feel anxious or worried about the future?

3. Does it take you a while to warm up to new people or circumstances? Would you say you are change averse?

4. Do you feel better knowing you have a plan for the worst that could happen?

5. Do you make decisions by committee, consulting several different people for their opinions beforehand?

6. When things are going well, are you the Chicken Little character who imagines that any minute now, the sky will fall in?

7. Do you have issues with authority figures, either challenging them on the one hand or putting too much faith in them on the other?

SNAP IDEAS FOR SIXES

Stop. Because your mind is terribly active and you're always planning for imminent disasters, it's hard for you to stay in the present moment. But I know plenty of Sixes who successfully work with SNAP. It will help you if you do it.

Notice. As you look around, what's going on? Are you overwhelmed because you've committed yourself to doing too many things? Notice

> Sixes are the most faithful and dependable people on the Enneagram.

whether there's anything you are feeling anxious about right now. Are you more or less worried or feeling more or less pessimistic than usual?

Observe your level of self-confidence. Are you asking a lot of people for advice or input to help you make a decision? Check to see whether you're having a "doubt" attack. If you're facing a decision, are you repeatedly toggling back and forth between two options?

Stand back and watch your mental activity. What are the conflicting voices in your brain currently saying?

Ask. As you learn more and more about your personality and the unique way you inhabit it, I encourage you to come up with your own questions more suited to your particular needs.

1. What am I believing right now? That I need to develop a contingency plan because something bad is surely going to happen? That the world is full of danger and people with hidden agendas? That I lack a reliable inner compass to guide me into making good decisions?

2. How does this make me feel? Worried? Pessimistic? Lacking self-confidence? Uncertain whether I should submit to or defy an authority figure?

3. Is it true? Is my world really such an insecure place? Is something bad always on the horizon? Does my personal history prove I'm less capable of making good decisions than other people? Is it *really* true?

4. What would my life be like if I let go of this belief? Would I have more faith and peace? Be less worried about making wrong decisions? Stop doubting the loyalty and steadfastness of the people who love me?

Pivot.

- To boost confidence and restore a positive outlook, write a list of past successes and positive outcomes.

- Stay out of the future and live in the present moment.

- When you make up your mind about something, resolve to stick to it.

- When worry and doubt strike, repeat Julian of Norwich's prayer, "All shall be well, and all shall be well, and all manner of thing shall be well."

Know that your life is held in the hands of a loving and competent God. Do something that reflects your conviction that God has your back. This will help cultivate faith, the contrary virtue of your deadly sin of fear.

%% %% %%

TYPE SEVEN

Hear What Sevens Have to Say

What I like about being a Seven:

People enjoy being around me and feel at ease with me. —Mary J.

Being able to innately find the goodness in things. —Lee Ann R.

What I don't like about being a Seven:

It's hard as a parent to be doing bedtime with kids and staying with routines. I've been a gypsy. I'm ready to go at a moment's notice. Health for me is when I'm contented to be at home with the kids. —Myra

A Seven-ish behavior:

As a teenager trying to escape the pain of my sister's death, falling in love was my drug of choice. I fell in love quickly and passionately, getting swept up in the emotion and the challenge. One relationship felt so intoxicating, so challenging, so deep that for a time I lost myself in it and there was never a dull moment. Loving him was a high. But when I started feeling controlled, the need for escape took over and I needed out. I didn't like being confined and having someone tell me what I could and couldn't do. A frightening and painful breakup sent me further into escaping by drinking, partying and casual sex. —Mary M.

What I wish other people understood about being a Seven:

I want people to know that Sevens may seem thick-skinned, but they can be very tenderhearted. Anytime we share our feelings, we are risking so much. Please be gentle with us. We need friends and family to walk alongside us through the dark places, and when we come across those places where no one can follow, knowing you are waiting for us on the other side can give us the courage to keep going. —Lee Ann R.

QUESTIONS TO HELP YOU FIGURE OUT WHETHER YOU ARE A SEVEN

1. In your earliest relationships, did you tend to be a commitment phobe? Is it difficult for you to commit to relationships?

2. Do you crave the excitement of planning an adventure, enjoying the anticipation as much as—or even more than—the actual event?

3. Are you a glass-half-full, sunny-side-up kind of person?

4. Do you try to avoid sad situations or people who are experiencing grief or pain?

5. Are you enticed by variety, spontaneity and change?

6. Do you often get your way by virtue of your considerable charm?

7. Would you agree that more is usually better?

SNAP IDEAS FOR SEVENS

Stop. Your spiritual gift is *not* stopping, so this will take some doing.

Here's what you need to know in advance: your mind will resist having to look at what's happening now because it's always somewhere out ahead of you in the future. You could run into unpleasant feelings in this exercise that might make you want to hightail out of it. You might find this practice predictable and routine after a while and want to move on to something else because it's boring. Remind yourself this practice can be as short or as long as you like.

Notice. Sevens suffer from "monkey mind." Your mind races and flits from one thought to the next, so be sure to take those deep breaths and get grounded in your body. What's going on in your body? Are you revved up, twitchy, tapping your foot or fingers?

> Sevens radiate joy and a love for life.

What's happening in the world around you at this moment? What are you and others doing? Have you missed anything that been happening?

Now notice what's happening in your mind. Are you planning a new escapade? Are you keeping yourself busier than usual? If so, are you aware of an unpleasant situation or feeling you're avoiding?

Are you having trouble focusing? Is there something you want to do or an item you'd like to own and you're having trouble resisting the temptation to do or buy whatever it is?

Are you feeling frustrated or impatient?

Ask. As you learn more and more about your personality and the unique way you inhabit it, I encourage you to come up with your own questions more suited to your particular needs.

1. What am I believing right now? That I'm alone and no one can be trusted to be there for me to help meet my needs? That happiness and satisfaction will only be found outside me and in the future? That I can avoid suffering if I devour enough interesting ideas, stay busy planning and anticipating new adventures, and always have an escape hatch? That I can reframe every negative into a positive or find the silver lining in any painful experience even when there isn't one?

2. Is it true? Am I really on my own? If I open myself up to having feelings like grief, boredom, sadness, disappointment or abandonment, will they overwhelm me? Is it *really* true?

3. How does that belief make me feel? Am I uncomfortable thinking about it for too long? Does it make me feel like I want to tell a funny story or point out the absurdity of this exercise? Does it make me long to be a deeper person?

4. What would my life be like if I let go of this belief? Would I be a deeper person? Would I finally be able to live in and enjoy the now? Would I enjoy deeper, more committed relationships with others?

Pivot.

• Memorize and repeatedly say the quotes, "Life is available only in the present moment" and "Smile, breathe, and go slowly." (These are both from Thich Nhat Hanh.)

• Delay gratification.

• Accept that life is limited, painful and boring at times.

• Stop negating feelings that make you feel uncomfortable.

• Take in and be grateful for what's here in this moment.

Choose your contrary virtue of sobriety over your deadly sin of gluttony by exercising self-restraint, staying in the present moment and being open to experiencing the full range of human emotions.

%%   %%   %%

QUESTIONS FOR REFLECTION AND DISCUSSION

Just to reiterate: if you are participating in a group that is discussing the Enneagram, it's important that you take the time to truly listen to what participants of other numbers have to say about themselves. Try to see the world through their eyes if possible. Allow them to speak without interruption. If you are going through this guide on your own, take time to reflect and journal through each question. Reflect on what it's like to be each number. The Enneagram is a great tool for developing empathy and compassion.

1. In this session we have been looking at the head triad: the Investigator, the Loyalist and the Enthusiast. If you are one of these three types, does the idea of leading with your instinct resonate with you? Why or why not?

2. Do the deadly sins associated with these numbers (avarice for Fives, fear for Sixes and gluttony for Sevens) ring true to you? What are spiritual practices that can counterbalance these deadly sins?

3. For Fives, Sixes and Sevens: What do you like most about your number?

4. For Fives, Sixes and Sevens: What do you like least about your number?

5. For Fives, Sixes and Sevens: What do you wish people understood about your number?

6. For people of the other six numbers: What do you most appreciate or envy about Fives, Sixes and Sevens?

7. For people of the other six numbers: What drives you crazy about Fives, Sixes and Sevens?

Reading for next week: chapter 12 of *The Road Back to You* and the wings material that relates to your number.

WORKING WITH YOUR TYPE

GOALS FOR THIS SESSION

• Explore your wings—the numbers on either side of yours

• Review the affirmations for each type

• Discuss your experiences in learning about the Enneagram

To read from *The Road Back to You*: chapter 12 and the wings material that relates to your number.

In this final session we'll wrap up what we've learned about our types, explore our wings and review our experiences with SNAP. Remember: the goal of developing self-awareness has been to learn when you're falling back into old self-limiting patterns and increase compassion for others (when you begin to understand why they are motivated to behave the way they do) and for yourself. Judging yourself harshly again and again never results in spiritual transformation; that only happens in an atmosphere of love.

EXPLORING YOUR WINGS

As you ponder your next steps with the Enneagram and strive to manage your particular type going forward, it can be helpful to pay more attention to the wings on either side of your

> When we privilege one of these nine characteristics above all else, that's when it becomes grotesque and unrecognizable or—let's just use the S word—sinful.

number. To remind you of the basic characteristics of each type, re-familiarize yourself with this list from the beginning of the book and think about which aspects of the types on either side of yours help describe your personality. It's also helpful to review the wings section in your type's chapter to see how different combinations play out.

Type One, the Perfectionist: Ethical, dedicated and reliable, they are motivated by a desire to live the right way, improve the world, and avoid fault and blame.

Type Two, the Helper: Warm, caring and giving, they are motivated by a need to be loved and needed, and to avoid acknowledging their own needs.

Type Three, the Performer: Success-oriented, image-conscious and wired for productivity, they are motivated by a need to be (or to appear to be) successful and avoid failure.

Type Four, the Romantic: Creative, sensitive and moody, they are motivated by a need to be understood, experience their feelings and avoid being ordinary.

Type Five, the Investigator: Analytical, detached and private, they are motivated by a need to gain knowledge, conserve energy and avoid relying on others.

Type Six, the Loyalist: Committed, practical and witty, they are worst-case-scenario thinkers who are motivated by fear and the need for security.

Type Seven, the Enthusiast: Fun, spontaneous and adventurous, they are motivated by a need to be happy, plan stimulating experiences and avoid pain.

Type Eight, the Challenger: Commanding, intense and confrontational, they are motivated by a need to be strong and avoid feeling weak or vulnerable.

Type Nine, the Peacemaker: Pleasant, diplomatic and accommodating, they are motivated by a need to keep the peace, merge with others and avoid conflict.

While your number doesn't change, you have access to the traits and resources of other numbers, and the ones most readily available are your wings. If you're a One with a Two wing, you have a reformer's drive to perfect the world but with the goal of helping others; if you're a Five with a Four wing, you have the Investigator's rich inner life complemented by the creativity (and the melancholy) of the Romantic. Think about and discuss whether you resonate more strongly with the type to the left or to the right of your number. (It may be both if you are bi-winged.)

APPRECIATING YOUR TYPE

Every number on the Enneagram reveals and teaches something about the character of the God who made us. Though not a comprehensive list, every number reveals a facet of God's nature. While each of us may tend to relate to or identify ourselves with one dimension of God's character more than others,

> God beholds us with the same soft gaze with which the adoring mother beholds her sleeping infant. If we could look at ourselves with that same quality of compassion, how much healing could take place in our souls?

we run into problems when we ascribe ultimate value to it. When we do, it turns something that was once beautiful into not only a grotesque caricature of itself but an idol as well. By fixating and attaching ourselves to one aspect of God's nature above all others, we reject and trade the wholeness God desires for us for the narrow confines of our personality.

With the Enneagram, part of the task ahead for you is to affirm and work toward health within your type. Part of the journey toward spiritual maturity in your number will come with simple and regular reminders. In your group or alone, compose an affirmation that will support you in your journey toward wholeness.

Type	Character of God	How We Distort That Characteristic
1	The goodness of God	By becoming perfectionists
2	The love of God	By becoming codependent
3	The glory of God	By promoting oneself
4	The beauty of God	By becoming self-absorbed
5	The omniscience of God	By becoming excessively detached
6	The steadfastness of God	By doubting excessively
7	The joy of God	By avoiding pain
8	The power of God	By becoming vengeful and controlling
9	The peace of God	By avoiding conflict

QUESTIONS FOR REFLECTION AND DISCUSSION

1. How would you describe yourself in terms of wings? Which characteristics of your wing type do you most recognize in yourself? Are there any that don't sound like you?

2. One of the quotations used for this session is "Every number on the Enneagram reveals and teaches something about the character of the God who made us." In what way do you think your number reflects some aspect of God?

3. In what ways do you distort or overemphasize this one trait to the exclusion of others? How does that spiritual myopia affect your understanding of God?

4. Which number do you *wish* you were on the Enneagram?

5. Which number do you still relate to the least on the Enneagram?

6. Have you been able to utilize SNAP to redirect an old behavior pattern? If so, describe that experience.

7. How will you implement what you've learned about the Enneagram in your relationships with others?

FURTHER READING

Appel, Wendy. *Inside Out Enneagram: The Game-Changing Guide for Leaders.* San Rafael, CA: Palma, 2001.

Baron, Renee, and Elizabeth Wagele. *The Enneagram Made Easy: Discover the Nine Types of People.* San Francisco: HarperOne, 1994.

Benner, David G. *The Gift of Being Yourself: The Sacred Call to Self-Discovery.* Downers Grove, IL: InterVarsity Press, 2004.

Brown, Brené. *The Gifts of Imperfection: Let Go of Who You Think You're Supposed to Be and Embrace Who You Are.* Center City, MN: Hazelden, 2010.

Campbell, Jocelyn. "Stance Keyword Checklist." Nine Paths: Exploring the Highways and Byways of the Enneagram. July 13, 2014. https://www.ninepaths.com/stance-keyword-checklist.

Chestnut, Beatrice M. *The Complete Enneagram: 27 Paths to Greater Self-Knowledge.* Berkeley, CA: She Writes, 2013.

Daniels, David N., and Virginia Ann Price. *The Essential Enneagram: The Definitive Personality Test and Self-Discovery Guide.* San Francisco: HarperSanFrancisco, 2000.

De Mello, Anthony. *The Way to Love: Meditations for Life.* New York: Image, 2013.

Horney, Karen. *Our Inner Conflicts: A Constructive Theory of Neurosis.* New York: Norton, 1992.

Howe-Murphy, Roxanne. *Deep Coaching: Using the Enneagram as a Catalyst for Profound Change.* El Granada, CA: Enneagram Press, 2007.

Hurley, Kathleen V., and Theodore Elliott Donson. *What's My Type? Use the Enneagram System of Nine Personality Types to Discover Your Best Self.* San Francisco: HarperSanFrancisco, 1991.

Kornfield, Jack. *A Path with Heart: A Guide Through the Perils and Promises of Spiritual Life.* New York: Bantam, 1993.

Levine, Janet. *The Enneagram Intelligences: Understanding Personality for Effective Teaching and Learning.* Westport, CT: Bergin & Garvey, 1999.

O'Malley, Mary. *The Gift of Our Compulsions: A Revolutionary Approach to Self-Acceptance and Healing.* Berkeley, CA: New World Library, 2010.

Palmer, Helen. *The Enneagram: Understanding Yourself and the Others in Your Life.* San Francisco: HarperSanFrancisco, 1991.

———. *The Enneagram in Love and Work: Understanding Your Intimate and Business Relationships.* San Francisco: HarperSanFrancisco, 1995.

———. *The Pocket Enneagram: Understanding the 9 Types of People.* San Francisco: HarperSanFrancisco, 1995.

Palmer, Helen, and Paul B. Brown. *The Enneagram Advantage: Putting the 9 Personality Types to Work in the Office.* New York: Three Rivers Press, 1997.

Pearce, Herb. *The Complete Idiot's Guide to the Power of the Enneagram.* Royersford, PA: Alpha, 2007.

Reynolds, Susan. *The Everything Enneagram Book: Identify Your Type, Gain Insight into Your Personality, and Find Success in Life, Love, and Business.* Avon, MA: F+W Media, 2010.

Rhodes, Susan. *The Positive Enneagram: A New Approach to the Nine Personality Types.* St. Louis: Geranium Press, 2009.

Riso, Don Richard, and Russ Hudson. *The Wisdom of the Enneagram: The Complete Guide to Psychological and Spiritual Growth for the Nine Personality Types.* New York: Bantam, 1999.

Rohr, Richard, and Andreas Ebert. *The Enneagram: A Christian Perspective.* New York: Crossroad, 2001.

Sheppard, Lynette. *The Everyday Enneagram: A Personality Map for Enhancing Your Work, Love, and Life—Every Day.* Petaluma, CA: Nine Points, 2000.

Zuercher, Suzanne. *Enneagram Spirituality: From Compulsion to Contemplation.* Notre Dame, IN: Ave Maria, 1992.

ALSO AVAILABLE

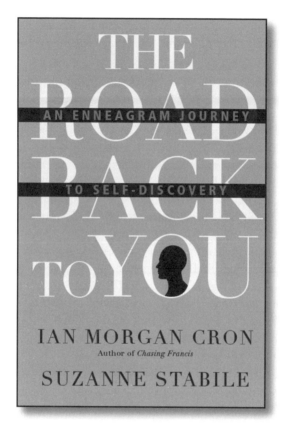

The Road Back to You:
An Enneagram Journey to Self-Discovery
978-0-8308-4619-1